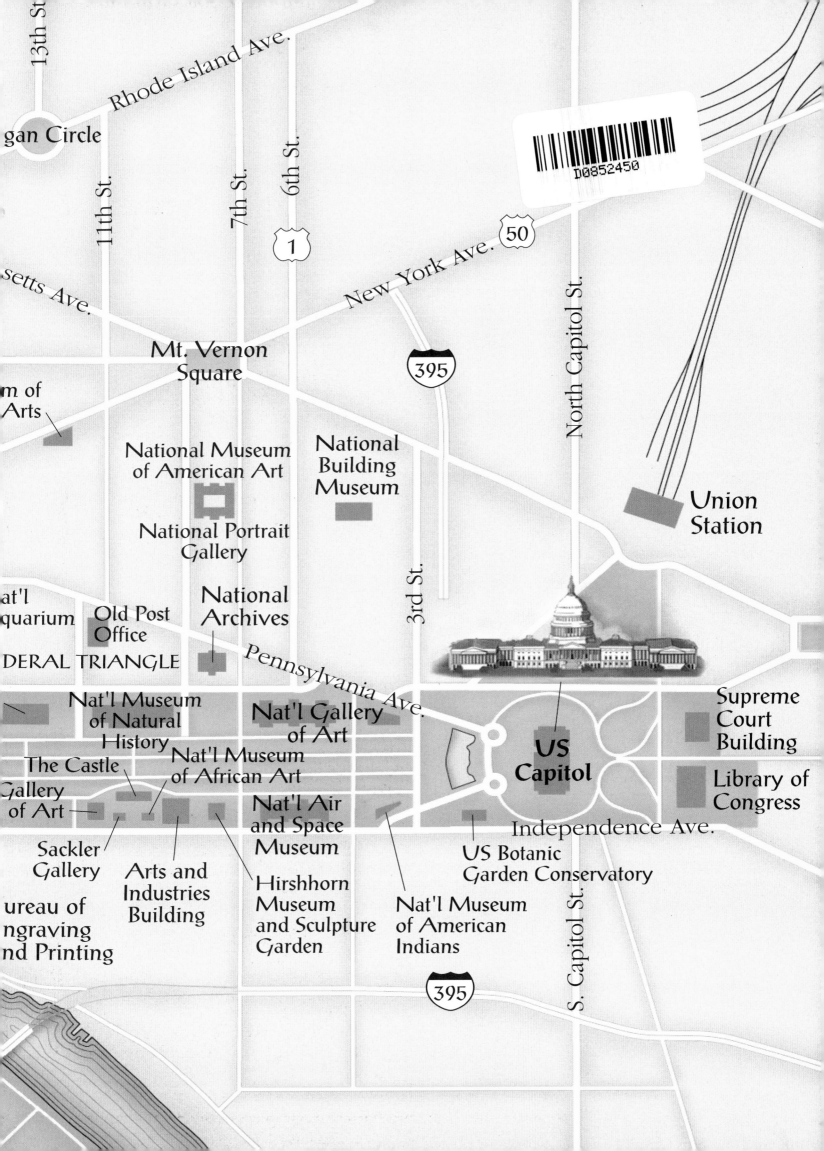

13th St.

Rhode Island Ave.

gan Circle

11th St.

7th St.

6th St.

(1)

setts Ave.

New York Ave. (50)

Mt. Vernon
Square

m of
Arts

(395)

National Museum
of American Art

National
Building
Museum

National Portrait
Gallery

North Capitol St.

Union
Station

at'l
quarium

Old Post
Office

National
Archives

3rd St.

DERAL TRIANGLE

Pennsylvania Ave.

US Capitol

Nat'l Museum
of Natural
History

Nat'l Gallery
of Art

Supreme
Court
Building

The Castle

Gallery
of Art

Nat'l Museum
of African Art

**US
Capitol**

Library of
Congress

Sackler
Gallery

Nat'l Air
and Space
Museum

Independence Ave.

ureau of
ngraving
nd Printing

Arts and
Industries
Building

Hirshhorn
Museum
and Sculpture
Garden

US Botanic
Garden Conservatory

Nat'l Museum
of American
Indians

S. Capitol St.

(395)

CAROL M. HIGHSMITH AND TED LANDPHAIR

WASHINGTON, D.C.

A PHOTOGRAPHIC TOUR

CRESCENT BOOKS

NEW YORK

THE AUTHORS GRATEFULLY ACKNOWLEDGE
THE SERVICES, ACCOMMODATIONS, AND SUPPORT PROVIDED BY
HILTON HOTELS CORPORATION
IN CONNECTION WITH THE COMPLETION OF THIS BOOK.

PAGE 1: *Planner Pierre L'Enfant described his Washington Mall as a "vast esplanade," along which he envisioned embassies, grand homes, and "all such sort of places as may be attractive to the learned and afford diversion to the idle." Today it lacks embassies and private homes, but the Smithsonian Institution complex, festivals, concerts, fireworks extravaganzas, softball games, and kite-flying expeditions provide ample diversion.* PAGES 2–3: *The White House, Washington Monument, and Jefferson Memorial present a stirring tableau at dusk. Once a miasmal bog and a tangle of bramble bushes, the lush ceremonial core of Washington today draws visitors from around the world.*

This 1997 edition is published by Crescent Books®, an imprint of Random House Value Publishing, Inc., 201 East 50th Street, New York, N.Y. 10022.

Crescent Books® and colophon are registered trademarks of Random House Value Publishing, Inc.

Random House
New York • Toronto • London • Sydney • Auckland
http://www.randomhouse.com/

Printed and bound in China

Library of Congress Cataloging-in-Publication Data
Highsmith, Carol M., 1946–
Washington, D. C. / Carol M. Highsmith and Ted Landphair.
  p. cm. — (A photographic tour)
ISBN 0-517-18460-5 (hc: alk. paper)
1. Washington (D.C.)—Tours. 2. Washington (D.C.)—Pictorial
works. I. Landphair, Ted, 1942– . II. Title. III. Series.
F192.3.H53 1997   96-27134
917.5304´4—dc20   CIP

12   11   10   9   8   7   6

Project Editor: Donna Lee Lurker
Designed by Robert L. Wiser, Archetype Press, Inc., Washington, D.C.

All photographs by Carol M. Highsmith unless otherwise credited: map by XNR Productions, page 5; painting by Frank Wright (photo from Washingtoniana Division, D.C. Public Library), page 6; National Park Service, page 8; Library of Congress, pages 9–20; Library of Congress and Columbia Historical Society, page 18; National Archives, page 19; National Theatre Archives, page 20; John F. Kennedy Memorial Library, page 21

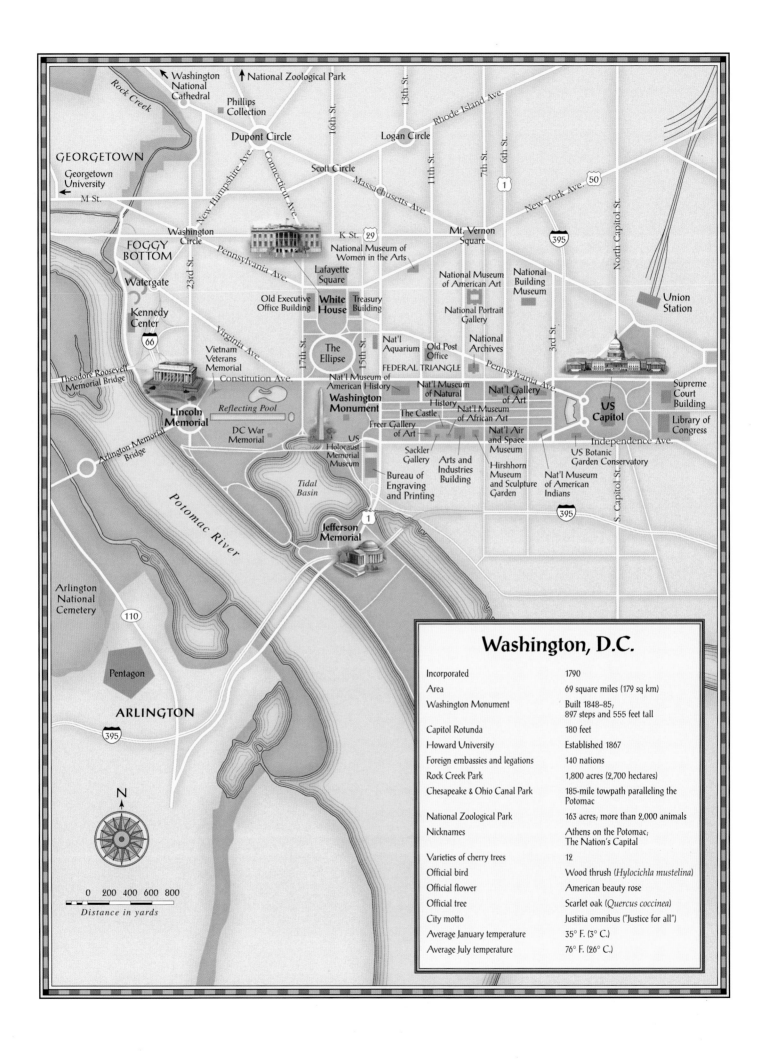

← Washington National Cathedral ↑ National Zoological Park

Rock Creek

Phillips Collection

16th St.

13th St.

Rhode Island Ave.

GEORGETOWN

Dupont Circle

Logan Circle

Georgetown University

M St.

Scott Circle

11th St.

7th St.

6th St.

Massachusetts Ave.

New York Ave. **50**

New Hampshire Ave.

Connecticut Ave.

1

Washington Circle

FOGGY BOTTOM

K St. **29**

Mt. Vernon Square

North Capitol St.

Watergate

Pennsylvania Ave.

National Museum of Women in the Arts

National Museum of American Art

National Building Museum

Union Station

Kennedy Center

66

23rd St.

Lafayette Square

Old Executive Office Building

White House

Treasury Building

National Portrait Gallery

395

Virginia Ave.

Vietnam Veterans Memorial

17th St.

The Ellipse

15th St.

Nat'l Aquarium

Old Post Office

National Archives

FEDERAL TRIANGLE

3rd St.

US Capitol

Theodore Roosevelt Memorial Bridge

Constitution Ave.

Nat'l Museum of American History

Pennsylvania Ave.

Supreme Court Building

Lincoln Memorial

Reflecting Pool

Washington Monument

Nat'l Museum of Natural History

Nat'l Gallery of Art

Library of Congress

DC War Memorial

The Castle

Nat'l Museum of African Art

US Capitol

Arlington Memorial Bridge

Freer Gallery of Art

Nat'l Air and Space Museum

Independence Ave.

US
Holocaust Memorial Museum

Sackler Gallery

Arts and Industries Building

Hirshhorn Museum and Sculpture Garden

US Botanic Garden Conservatory

Nat'l Museum of American Indians

Potomac River

Tidal Basin

Bureau of Engraving and Printing

1

395

S. Capitol St.

Jefferson Memorial

1

Arlington National Cemetery

110

Pentagon

ARLINGTON

395

N

0 200 400 600 800
Distance in yards

Washington, D.C.

Incorporated	1790
Area	69 square miles (179 sq km)
Washington Monument	Built 1848–85; 897 steps and 555 feet tall
Capitol Rotunda	180 feet
Howard University	Established 1867
Foreign embassies and legations	140 nations
Rock Creek Park	1,800 acres (2,700 hectares)
Chesapeake & Ohio Canal Park	185-mile towpath paralleling the Potomac
National Zoological Park	163 acres; more than 2,000 animals
Nicknames	Athens on the Potomac; The Nation's Capital
Varieties of cherry trees	12
Official bird	Wood thrush (*Hylocichla mustelina*)
Official flower	American beauty rose
Official tree	Scarlet oak (*Quercus coccinea*)
City motto	Justitia omnibus ("Justice for all")
Average January temperature	35° F. (3° C.)
Average July temperature	76° F. (26° C.)

IT HAS BEEN CALLED AMERICA'S LAST COMPANY TOWN. If so, it's certainly the most beautiful, the last alabaster city still gleaming. Fletcher Knebel called it "democracy's home town," where decisions bear directly on lives everywhere. Ben Bagdikian said it was "the home office of the nation." When John F. Kennedy came to town in 1960, he observed wryly that it was a city of "southern efficiency and northern charm." Then a dozy metropolitan area of two million people, by the 1990s it had grown into a region of four and one half million people, with seven times more private-sector workers than federal bureaucrats. The region could boast five of the nation's top-ten "edge cities," that is, suburbs or nearby towns. It could claim forty of *Inc.* magazine's five hundred fastest-growing companies, the country's highest percentage of working women, and its second-largest number of technology companies. It also generated well over half of America's overseas Internet traffic and had the highest percentage of scientists, engineers, and people over twenty-five with college degrees. The area enjoys the most museums (more than fifty) and art galleries (seventy-plus), the most per-capita public performances of the arts, and nearly ninety thousand areas that are protected from development.

Tourists come, just as they had in the 1950s when Dorothea Jones coined the phrase, because the air in Washington is still "thick with history." James Madison wrote a provision into the new Constitution that the federal government would be located in a capital that was not part of any state. Secretary of State Thomas Jefferson won a southern locale for the new capital city in return for a promise from southern states that they would help pay the Revolutionary War debts of all former colonies. The chosen spot was a diamond-shaped, one hundred-square-mile chunk of Maryland and Virginia. Straddling the Potomac River, this new "District of Columbia" encompassed not only a new capital city, carved out of some of the thickest woods and foulest swamps north of Georgia, but also the bustling, independent river cities of Alexandria and Georgetown. More attractive sites, farther up the Potomac River, had been proposed, but this land was close to the Mount Vernon estate of President Washington, and that sealed the deal.

George Washington commissioned Major Pierre-Charles L'Enfant, an inveterate dreamer, to design the Federal City in 1792. His sketches laid out a logical grid, interrupted by wide boulevards, squares and circles, and slashing radials reminiscent of his native Paris, and what he called a "vast esplanade," which we now know as the Washington Mall, inspired by Versailles. The "Plan of the City of Washington" turned murky Tiber Creek into a splendid canal up which he envisioned each new president floating for his inauguration. The hotheaded L'Enfant was fired before the job was finished, and American surveyors Andrew Ellicott and Benjamin Banneker finished laying out the new capital. But when the new government moved to town from Philadelphia in 1800, the ceremonial core had only one muddy road—Pennsylvania Avenue, which a newspaper soon called a "Serbonian bog." Connecticut Congressman John Cotton Smith took one look at the new capital and proclaimed it "a deep morass covered with elder bushes." The British ambassador packed up and went home rather than serve in such a hardship post.

Hot, humid, and malarial, the nation's capital never evolved into the bustling center of manufacturing and commerce that General Washington had envisioned. Indeed, it grew so slowly that Congress ceded back the Virginia portion in 1846. Right up to the Civil War, much of the land remained a "pestiferous swamp." Charles Dickens, visiting in 1842, wrote home to London about "spacious avenues that begin in nothing and lead nowhere; streets a mile long that only want houses, roads, and inhabitants; public buildings that need but a public to be complete."

Washington lay well out of sight of the Mason-Dixon line, and it was clearly slave territory.

Franklin Delano Roosevelt's third inauguration on January 20, 1941, was full of the usual pomp—with added gravity. The inaugural parade was a show of wartime preparedness as color-bearers marched in combat uniforms, not parade dress. Hundreds of tanks followed marching units up Pennsylvania Avenue.

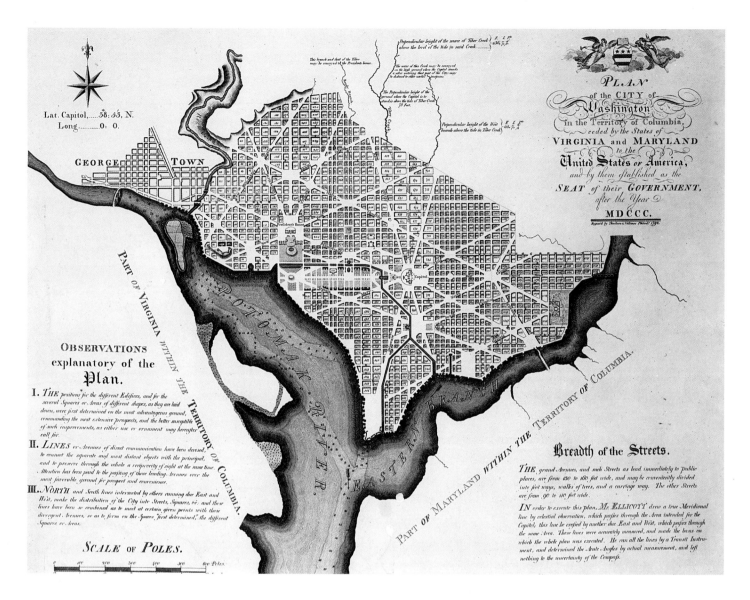

The 1792 Plan of the City of Washington shows a logical grid, interrupted by diagonal boulevards and an unimpeded vista between the White House and the Capitol. The Treasury Department Building would later spoil the view.

Free black laborers had helped build L'Enfant's first avenues, but by 1840 the Saint Charles Hotel, three blocks from the Capitol, was touting its slave pens in the basement, and gangs of human chattel were shoved to auction down Pennsylvania Avenue. After the Civil War, however, thousands of freed slaves moved to Washington. The city became a laboratory for black empowerment with the Freedmen's Bureau, Freedmen's Hospital, and the founding of Howard University in 1867 to serve a growing black population. In 1871, when the Republican Congress set up an elected territorial government for "the District"—as locals then and now call the City of Washington—it included several blacks. It was not until the 1920s, with the advent of Jim Crow laws throughout the South, that segregation took firm hold in Washington theaters, restaurants, libraries, and the baseball field (but not the stands) at Griffith Stadium. Nonetheless, the New Deal that opened thousands of civil-service and military jobs to blacks brought another mass migration that produced a thriving black middle class and the first black high school in America.

The Constitution had given Congress the power to govern Washington, and when it established an elected territorial government in 1871 it was the city's first brief fling at home rule. Territorial governor Alexander "Boss" Shepherd mobilized more than $6 million in public improvements, including the planting of fifty thousand trees, the laying of twenty-three miles of sewers, and the conversion of B Street—under which ran the odiferous remnants of the city canal—into an imposing boulevard. In 1932, on George Washington's two-hundredth birthday, this thoroughfare would become Constitution Avenue. But Shepherd ran up debts of more than $16 million, was branded corrupt by Congress, and fled to Mexico in disgrace. So much for home rule. Shepherd, though, returned for a hero's parade down Pennsylvania Avenue in 1887; John Philip Sousa led the Marine Band, and "three cheers for the maker of Washington!" rang from a crowd one hundred thousand strong.

More than eighty years later, in the wake of the civil-rights movement of the 1960s and the riots in 1968 that followed the assassination of Dr. Martin Luther King Jr., Washington, by then 70 percent black, got a tepid taste of self-determination once again—tepid because Congress retained the power of a thirty-day veto of any new city laws. Charles C. Diggs, a black Democrat from Michigan and chairman of the House District of Columbia Committee, steered through a new home-rule charter that gave the city the right to elect local officials. At last, he proclaimed, Washingtonians would be "masters of their fate." But the result over the next quarter-century was anything but a model. Three mayors presided over a steady erosion in city services, the ballooning of political-patronage jobs, and deepening budget deficits. In 1974, Walter E. Washington, the last appointed mayor-commissioner, was elected mayor. Genial and benign, he was viewed with suspicion by the city's population as a tool of the largely white Board of Trade. When Marion Barry, once a community radical and friend of Dr. King's, replaced Washington in 1979 and brought into government a cadre of idealists and technocrats, the city flowered for a time. It began to run annual surpluses and pay down its onerous deficit. Middle-class blacks and whites alike ventured back to the city and began restoring neighborhoods around the beautiful circles. Wretched stretches of urban blight along Pennsylvania Avenue and the Georgetown waterfront began a slow turnaround into architectural showplaces, full of life both day and night. With Barry's re-election came an epidemic of cockiness, complacency, largess to friendly contractors, and generous raises for city workers. His term of office ended abruptly in 1990 when the FBI videotaped him smoking crack cocaine, a crime for which he was sent to federal prison for six months.

Sharon Pratt Kelly, elected mayor in 1990, became the first black female mayor of a large American city. Though her administration began with high hopes, little changed. She was trounced in a bid for re-election and virtually disappeared from public view. Pronouncing himself "rejuvenated," Marion Barry, who after his release from prison had won a council seat in Anacostia, the city's bleakest ward, ran for and won back his old job as mayor. But he faced a daunting task. The spread of crack cocaine was escalating the violence on city streets, and once again the middle class of all races began to depart the city, leaving it to the disgruntled wealthy and the ever-needier poor. All the while, the federal government was moving more and more agencies—including the National Bureau of Standards, a new National Archives annex, the National Science Foundation, and many functions of the National Weather Service—to the suburbs. Home rule had burdened the city with many responsibilities of a state, including backbreaking Medicaid payments, half the costs of welfare, a prison soon packed to overcrowding, and an unfunded pension debt that topped $4 million by the mid-1990s. The only trappings of a state that the District seemingly could afford were

L'Enfant's "magnificent spaces" were soon crowded with peddlers like the itinerant farmer in this 1839 view. In 1872 the city would get a giant one-stop shopping center, Center Market, which filled three blocks on Pennsylvania Avenue.

The White House was easily accessible in 1830 when Andrew Jackson occupied it. "Let the people rule" had been his campaign slogan, and he frequently opened his home to crowds of backwoods supporters.

an official flower (the American Beauty rose) and official bird (the wood thrush). The city was shackled by an artificially constrained tax base. Two of every three dollars earned there were carried home by nonresidents who by federal law could not be taxed, and 50 percent of the land was either federal property or in the hands of nonprofit (but often exceedingly wealthy) corporations exempt from city taxation. Nor could the considerable property of foreign governments be touched by the tax collector.

Washington was left with the highest combined federal and local income- and sales-tax rate of any American city save New York. Cars were booted and parking citations zealously written, strictly for the revenue. Toward the millennium's end only a little over 10 percent of city taxpayers earned more than $50,000 annually, but they shouldered almost half the income taxes. As former U.S. Housing Secretary Jack Kemp pointed out, Washington's dire fiscal condition produced a "vicious cycle of middle-class flight, job destruction as businesses leave for the suburbs, increasing demands for public assistance, and a shrinking tax base." The fact that all this took place in a world capital magnified the humiliation. But poverty, crime, drugs, and homelessness were not unique to Washington. They had become the earmarks of many center cities.

Yet in the face of it all, thousands of middle-class and wealthy Washingtonians stayed. Why? Simple, they said. Because the city remained a great place to live. In a *Washington Post* op-ed column, local speechwriter Budd Whitebook waxed optimistic. "The real charms of Washington are unofficial, organic," he wrote. "And often accidental, like coming across two ferociously engaged fencers one evening by the Potomac near Hains Point . . . or like the springtime explosion of azaleas along Reno Road."

The city still had much to offer. A lavish housing stock; eighty-five hundred acres of city

green spaces, including Rock Creek Park, the country's first and largest urban parkland; a vibrant and growing array of dance clubs, sports bars, sidewalk festivals, farmers' markets, coffee bars, and unparalleled cultural attractions like the Kennedy Center for the Performing Arts, the Smithsonian Institution complex, and the world's foremost Shakespeare collection at the Folger Shakespeare Library all remained close at hand. Three hours away, the ocean; two, the Blue Ridge Mountains; one, the rich Chesapeake Bay. Just across state lines in Virginia and Maryland lay gourmet inns, an antiquers' paradise, outlet malls, orchards, fishing holes, rocks to climb, and great golf.

Though the District's morale was deflated by Washington Redskins owner Jack Kent Cooke's decision to take his football team to the suburbs, it was buoyed by word that Abe Pollin, owner of the hockey Capitals and basketball Bullets, would be moving his operations in the opposite direction. A new twenty-thousand-seat sports arena, the MCI Center, named for one of the largest remaining Washington-based corporations, would occupy a slice of the grim Gallery Place neighborhood near Chinatown in time for the 1997–98 basketball and hockey seasons. The good news was compounded in 1996 by President Clinton's signature on a bill enabling pre-construction of a new convention center in the six-city-block area north of the existing undersized facility. Once a favorite convention city, Washington had been bypassed by most convention planners in favor of gigantic complexes in New Orleans, Las Vegas, New York, Orlando, and Chicago. The new D.C. facility, costing $450 million and offering 800,000 square feet of exhibition space, was expected to move the nation's capital back into the top ten in convention business, and none too soon. By the mid-1990s, more than twenty million people a year visited Washington. More than half came purely for pleasure, but business travel was also increasing.

The U.S. Capitol of 1812—two years before the British would torch it—is barely recognizable without the dome and lower, wider House and Senate chambers that would replace these towers.

Washington's array of historic and cultural sites still holds a strong attraction for tourists, and recent years have seen many new additions to perennial favorites like the Washington Monument and President Washington's home at Mount Vernon. In fact, a dazzling new Pennsylvania Avenue facelift was so successful that the public-private Pennsylvania Avenue Development Corporation declared its job done and went out of business. The last hole in Pennsylvania Avenue's monolithic Federal Triangle was filled with the completion of a gargantuan international cultural and trade building—the largest public building in America after the Pentagon. It is across the street from the city's oldest cultural institution, the 1835-vintage National Theatre. An army of jobless men had built the Triangle, a procession of limestone, tile-roofed Beaux-Arts federal agency buildings, as part of Franklin Roosevelt's New Deal Works Progress Administration during the Great Depression. The monoliths displaced venerable remnants of downtown Washington: Center Market, with its three-block array of butchers, fishmongers, greengrocers, dry-goods dealers, and eating houses; the arcane Southern Railway Building; Harvey's oyster house, once Abraham Lincoln's favorite eatery; Poli's Theater, called "as ugly outside as it was beautiful within; brothels and ale houses left over from the days when the section was called "Murder Row"; and old warehouses where Bonus Army marchers squatted in 1932 before they were routed by the tanks of General Douglas MacArthur. The 1899 Old Post Office building, the city's first steel-frame structure, survived then and again in the 1970s when blight-fighters tried to tear it down. The *New York Times* had mocked the enormous Gothic structure as "a cross between a cathedral and a cotton mill," but citizens loved it. It became a popular shopping mall, office building, food court, and drop-off point for tour buses.

But few malls anywhere in America occupy quarters as historic as the one at Union Station,

Work continued right through the Civil War on Charles Bulfinch's copper-sheathed wooden Capitol dome. Washington was a staging ground for the vast Union Army, which, to President Lincoln's dismay, paraded far more smartly than it fought for many years.

a few blocks up Louisiana Avenue from the U.S. Capitol. Rising above the sewery remains of Tiber Creek in a roughneck Irish shantytown called "Swampoodle" in 1907, monolithic Union Station was the creation of Daniel H. Burnham, master architect of the epic 1893 World's Columbian Exposition in Chicago. By 1928, more than three hundred trains a day would pull into and out of the shed behind the terminal's vaulted Great Hall filled with Constantinian arches, egg-and-dart molding, sunstreaked gilt leafing, majestic skylights, and Louis Saint-Gaudens' twenty-five-ton statues of Roman Centurions. The ticketing and boarding concourse was spacious enough to hold America's standing army (then fifty thousand strong) or the full Washington Monument laid on its side. So heavy was foot traffic that in 1945 a red-cap told of accepting bribes to put people in wheelchairs, just so they could cut through the crowds to the trains. But with the advent of air travel, Union Station, like all American passenger-train terminals, fell into terrible disrepair. At its sorriest moment, someone came up with the idea of turning the humongous station into a National Visitor Center. A hole—scornfully dubbed "The Pit"—was gouged in the Main

The opulent Willard Hotel was the social center of Washington around 1860 and for many decades to follow. Several presidents and nearly every visiting notable stayed there.

Hall's terrazzo floor, into which tourists could descend by escalator to view a slide show about Washington attractions that they could see just as well by walking out the front door. At one point, Senator Daniel Patrick Moynihan wondered aloud whether the same number of people who descended into The Pit eventually emerged. Ridicule and unrelenting leaks in the roof doomed the National Visitor Center. Mushrooms sprouted in abandoned offices upstairs, and in 1981 the center closed for good. But a remarkable coalition—including the U.S. Department of the Interior; Amtrak, the nation's new passenger-rail carrier whose zippy new Metroliner trains were reviving rail travel throughout the Northeast; and a quasi-public redevelopment agency— brought together artisans and laborers who stunningly restored America's frowsy *grande dame* of surface transportation. It helped that the city's regional transit agency brought in its shiny new Metro subway line to meet the trains, as the remarkably clean, efficient, and safe city rail system was already a bonafide tourist attraction in itself. Out on the old concourse rose three shopping levels, and on a Wednesday night in September 1988, three thousand of Washington's *haute monde* helped dedicate the refurbished terminal. It would soon become a fully operational Amtrak, subway, and commuter-rail hub as well.

Years later and more than a mile away, the Korean War Veterans Memorial opened on seven and one half acres of the National Mall, across the Reflecting Pool from the intensely moving Vietnam Veterans Memorial. The more than fifty-eight thousand American dead of the Vietnam War are memorialized, name by name, on Maya Lin's polished granite wall. Soon known simply as "The Wall," the memorial helped national healing over the fiercely divisive war and became a focal point of profound contemplation. Some visitors bring paper and pencil to rub the name of a loved one. Others leave mementos—photographs, dog tags, shoes, even a "tiger cage" in which one man had been imprisoned.

U.S. veterans of the earlier United Nations "police action" on the Korean Peninsula had been virtually forgotten, as had the conflict itself almost the moment it ended. But they are remembered today at the Korean War Veterans Memorial, which was completed in 1995. The memorial combines nineteen freestanding stainless-steel troopers in ponchos, depicted as

Even suburbanites took the streetcar to Center Market in the 1890s. Run for a time by the U.S. Department of Agriculture itself, the market featured a long indoor pavilion where the National Archives Building now stands.

trudging cautiously through a rice paddy toward an American flag. To one side is a polished-granite wall far different from that of the Vietnam Veterans Memorial across the way. Instead of the names of the dead, there are etched faces, taken from actual archival photographs, of more than twenty-five hundred nurses, mechanics, pilots, Seabees, and other support troops so critical to the preservation of democracy in southern Korea.

The United States Holocaust Memorial Museum also provides an opportunity for sober reflection. Opened in 1993, it is across from the Washington Monument at Independence Avenue and Fifteenth Street, renamed Raoul Wallenberg Place for the Swedish diplomat who saved nearly one hundred thousand Budapest Jews from Nazi extermination during World War II. The museum presents the history of the persecution and murder of six million Jews, homosexuals, Gypsies, and other victims of Nazi tyranny from 1933 to 1945. Before touring its permanent exhibition, visitors receive identity cards bearing the names, pictures, and histories of Holocaust victims of their sex and approximate age. The most gruesome images and artifacts are displayed behind "privacy walls."

Not that National Park Service rangers were often idle at Washington's older symbolic monuments: the Lincoln Memorial, Washington Monument, and Jefferson Memorial. Robert Mills's Washington Monument towers more than 555 feet high above the Washington Mall. President James K. Polk laid the cornerstone in an 1848 ceremony attended by Representatives Abraham Lincoln and Andrew Johnson, but funds to build the obelisk, collected from popular subscriptions by the Washington Monument Society, ran out in 1853. It stood unfinished for nearly a quarter-century until President Ulysses S. Grant approved an act authorizing completion. Thus sharp-eyed visitors can detect a difference in coloration of the marble façade at the 152-foot level. In 1884, a thirty-three-hundred-pound marble capstone was placed on the Washington Monument and topped with a nine-inch pyramid of cast aluminum, then a rare metal. For years only men were permitted to take the elevator to the monument's observation deck. Women and children were asked to trudge up the 897 steps because the elevator was considered "too dangerous." Today, the views out four small windows high in the monument—and from the top of the Old Post Office tower across the Mall—are still the most panoramic that are readily accessible to the public.

The Lincoln Memorial, built on landfill called West Potomac Park that extended L'Enfant's National Mall, was designed by architect Henry Bacon and dedicated in 1922. Daniel Chester French's nineteen-foot-high statue of Lincoln, looking out toward the Potomac River, is made of twenty-eight interlocking blocks of Georgia marble. The memorial's thirty-six Doric columns represent the states of the Union at the time of Lincoln's death. Above the frieze are the names and entry dates into the Union of the forty-eight states when the memorial was completed. (Latecoming Alaska and Hawaii get a mention in an inscription chiseled into the building's terrace.) Architect John Russell Pope's Jefferson Memorial on the Potomac Tidal Basin directly south of the White House, dedicated in 1943 on the two-hundredth anniversary of the third president's birth, completed the monumental heart of Washington. The circular colonnaded structure was adapted from the classical style that Jefferson himself introduced to the country. Rudulph Evans sculpted the bronze statue in the center of the memorial, which gets its heaviest visitation in early spring, when three thousand cherry trees, a gift from the people of Japan in 1912, bloom throughout the Tidal Basin.

Because of Abraham Lincoln's life and shocking death at the hands of John Wilkes Booth, the Lincoln Memorial and Ford's Theater, where Lincoln was felled, have long been secular shrines. And for the more than four million people who visit annually, Arlington National Cemetery, across Memorial Bridge from Lincoln's monument, has also been a solemn place of homage—a spot to walk among the almost two hundred and fifty thousand headstones of veterans and their dependents buried on 612 acres of land. The Tomb of the Unknowns from four American wars is guarded twenty-four hours a day by sentinels from the "Old Guard," the U.S. 3d Infantry. Many visitors pause at the graves of John and Jackie Kennedy, and at that of Robert Kennedy, who are buried there. Adjacent to the cemetery is Arlington House, the home of Robert E. and Mary Custis Lee. Confiscated by Union troops during the Civil War for use as a headquarters and military cemetery—the first two hundred acres of what became Arlington National Cemetery—the estate was used by the War Department during World War I, then by cemetery administrators and park service officials until 1955, when the mansion became a memorial to General Lee.

For a cultural stew of art, history, and science, no other American experience compares with a prolonged visit to the complex of Smithsonian Institution museums, most of which are anchored along the Mall and Independence Avenue. The first national organization for the promotion of arts and sciences was chartered by Congress in 1818, but its holdings consisted of only a small museum of botany and mineralogy, plus a garden. Then James Smithson, a British scientist and gambler who had never visited the United States, bequeathed

Pennsylvania Avenue has been called "America's Main Street." It was certainly the city's business hub at the turn of the century, before a wall of giant federal buildings turned it into a bureaucratic canyon.

$500,000—a small fortune at the time—to the young democratic republic across the sea for scientific research and the establishment of a museum bearing his name. The bequest was conditional on his youngest survivor, a nephew, dying without an heir. Fortunately for the American nation, and for Smithson's fame, the nephew obliged. The Smithsonian administration building, the reddish-brown sandstone Gothic "Castle," was designed by American architect James Renwick in 1852. The first museum, the Arts and Industries Building, opened in 1881. Its most popular exhibits, the United States flag that waved defiantly at the British from Fort McHenry in 1814, and an array of First Ladies' gowns, would later become mainstays of the institution's National Museum of American History, just as Colonel Charles Lindbergh's famous *Spirit of St. Louis* airplane, which dangled in a hallway, would be moved to the new Air and Space Museum. Today, the old Arts and Industries Building still displays the wonders of the 1876 Philadelphia Centennial Exposition. One of Washington's most famous meeting spots is beneath the giant stuffed African bush elephant in the rotunda of the National Museum of Natural History, which opened in 1910. Hidden from view to this day as the public passes displays of animals, rocks, and human antiquities—not to mention the Hope Diamond—are vast warrens of researchers studying anthropology, biology, and geology and sending forth expeditions.

The most visited museum in the world, according to the Smithsonian, is the Air and Space Museum, which opened in 1976. Its twenty-three galleries display aircraft from both world wars, U.S. spacecraft, the Wright Brothers' 1903 flyer, and Lucky Lindy's plane. The Smithsonian complex has also grown to include seven galleries devoted to American, Asian, African, and modern art; the National Postal Museum; one of the world's great zoos; and even two museums in New York City. In the early 1990s, ground was broken for a new National Museum of the American Indian across Fourth Street from the Air and Space Museum. The Smithsonian, which marked one hundred and fifty years of free access, spent a year in the early 1990s studying the possibility of charging admission fees but concluded they would "breach an institutional tradition."

The Smithsonian was once an official repository of American books in print—not just on science and art but also on literature, poetry, and a variety of other subjects. In the years immediately before the Civil War, the institution's librarian, Charles Coffin Jewett, floated the idea of creating a new national library—not surprisingly under his control—in which to house this rapidly expanding collection. Instead, Congress ordered the works shipped across the Mall to its own Library of Congress, which by then had already become the nation's *de facto* national library via massive purchases and donations through the copyright process. Today the Library of Congress is the world's preeminent collection of human thought and creativity—not just in books but also on film, maps, photographs, sheet music, phonographic records and tapes, computer disks, and an eclectic array of copyright submissions that range from soup labels to the original Kewpie Doll. The ornate headquarters building, named for Thomas Jefferson, opened in 1897 when the Library's collections were moved out of overstuffed rooms and corridors in the Capitol dome. Its own gold dome—and its Main Reading Room filled with symbolic statues, granite busts, epic paintings, Pompeiian panels, and bas-reliefs—became a temple of knowledge and an immediate tourist attraction. So overwhelming had the Library of

The White House Easter-egg roll goes back at least to 1898, when renowned female photographer Frances Benjamin Johnston captured this shot. William McKinley, who presided, was one of five presidents who sat for Johnston portraits.

Congress become, with its twenty million books—three-fourths in 460 languages other than English—and ninety-five million items in formats *other* than books, that Congress began to wonder, as the turn of the century neared, whether it should rein in the Library's scope by limiting it to domestic acquisitions, restrict access to governmental inquiries, or try to find the funds to maintain its status as the world's central storehouse for the Information Age.

Congress gets its own share of visitors, of course, though heightened security aroused by terrorist incidents at home and abroad means tourists can no longer stroll into the U.S. Capitol and wander the halls and visitors' gallery at will. In the years that work was interrupted on the Washington Monument, construction continued unabated on the Capitol. Completion of the cast-iron dome in 1863 moved President Lincoln to state, "If people see the Capitol going on, it's a sign we intend the Union shall go on." Pierre L'Enfant had carefully selected the new capital city's highest point, Jenkins Hill, for the "Congress House," and work began on the building well before the government moved to Washington. President Washington visited in 1793 to lay the cornerstone, marching ankle-deep in powdery soil up Pennsylvania Avenue at the head of a parade of Masons to do so. A year earlier William Thornton, a physician and amateur architect from the West Indies, had won a national competition for the capitol's design. Not much was in place when the U.S. Senate and U.S. House of Representatives moved in, but by 1806 an imposing House wing was completed. British troops torched the temporary wooden walkways and most of the Capitol's contents (including the holdings of the new Library of Congress) during the War of 1812, but it was rebuilt and greatly expanded under the supervision of architect Benjamin Latrobe. Four columns salvaged from the fire were incorporated into the New Capital Hotel on Pennsylvania Avenue. As the Capitol grew, its low, wooden dome was replaced by a

Why waste manpower or fuel, went the reasoning during World War I, when sheep can keep the White House lawn trim? Then and during World War II, the military jammed the Ellipse behind the White House with temporary buildings.

twin-shelled, nine-million-ton cast-iron dome. Sculptor Thomas Crawford created *Freedom,* the nineteen-foot-high, seven-and-one-half-ton bronze statue that stands atop the dome. The statue is often mistakenly called "Pocahontas" by tourists and tour guides alike. The chambers, anterooms, and hallways of the Capitol are adorned with imposing statuary depicting states-men—and women—from each state, and astonishingly beautiful murals, friezes, ceiling frescos, and paintings.

Up Pennsylvania Avenue, where L'Enfant's planned clear line of sight to the White House was interrupted when Congress and President Jackson plopped the Treasury Building in the way, the president's home also gets a steady stream of well-watched visitors. George Washing-ton had also laid the cornerstone of the house designed by architect James Hoban, but he never lived there. John Adams moved in when Congress came to town in 1800. British troops set the presidential mansion aflame in 1814 as well, and only a drenching thunderstorm on the second evening prevented a citywide conflagration. It was after the charred planks of James and Dol-ley Madison's home were repainted that it became known as the "White House." Ever since, the public has treasured the building, even if some presidents did not (Harry Truman called it "a great white prison"). Getting in unescorted was once easy. After Jackson took the presidential oath in 1829, Old Hickory invited the whole roaring mob of backwoods supporters in for a drink. They promptly mashed food and whiskey into the silk damask upholstery and scattered the remains of a fourteen-hundred-pound wheel of cheese. Later public access became a morn-ing ritual of long queues in rain, snow, or sunshine. The tour was made more comfortable in 1995 with the opening of a White House Visitors' Center, complete with exhibits and restrooms, across the street in the Commerce Department Building.

Presidents have traveled up Pennsyl-vania Avenue in life and death, and the avenue has seen parades of wartime heroes, suffragists, Ku Klux Klansmen, Bonus Marchers, and these supporters of "Be Kind of Animals Week" in 1920.

The highest order of the nation's third branch of government, the U.S. Supreme Court, did not get a building of its own until 1935. Justices met in the Capitol for many years and even, for a time, in a local tavern. Architect Cass Gilbert designed the marble temple to the law, in which the high court convenes from the first Monday in October until the session's caseload is completed, usually in June.

Lobbying is a Washington artform, of course, but the term did not originate on Capitol Hill. Nor did it first refer to professional influence brokers. It was coined to describe the cluster of citizens who congregated at Washington's "Hotel of Presidents," the Willard on Pennsylvania Avenue, in the 1870s. President Ulysses S. Grant would stroll over from the White House, pull up a chair, take out a cigar, and listen to the complaints and job entreaties of loiterers in the lobby. The list of the nation's prominent who did *not* stay at the Willard seemed shorter than those who did. Charles Dickens and Mark Twain did. So did the Marquis de Lafayette, Phineas T. Barnum, and Julia Ward Howe. Calvin Coolidge spent his entire vice presidency there. On a hot, sleepless August night in 1963, Martin Luther King Jr. put the final touches on a

Just before the official announcement, this family read all about the Japanese surrender in 1945. The Evening Star Building is in the background. That great daily newspaper is gone, and its renovated building is an office tower.

speech he was to deliver to cap off the Poor People's March on Washington the following day. The added language began, "I have a dream." Like many old downtown hotels, the Willard declined precipitously in the 1950s and '60s. It was closed, most of its contents sold at auction, and set for demolition before a remarkable citizen coalition managed to stave off the wrecking ball. In 1978, developers restored and reappointed the Willard as a luxury hotel.

Every week in Washington, it seems, a new museum, exhibit, or tour tantalizes the public. Overdosed on reptiles at the zoo, rockets at Air and Space, and Renoirs at the National Gallery of Art? Try the National Gallery of Caricature and Cartoon Art, a remarkable collection of forty-five thousand cartoons by three thousand artists. Or the "Pollinarium," examining pollination in the zoo's greenhouse. There's no worry about crowds at the Franciscan monastery, the Department of State's diplomatic reception rooms, the Voice of America's studios, and the Washington National Cathedral's daily "tour and tea." Even tour buses are passé. Electric boats called "water buses" stop at two memorials, the Georgetown waterfront, and Theodore Roosevelt Island. And tourists can hop into a three-wheeled, human-powered "pedicab" at four locations.

Visitors gravitate not just to museums and memorials, but also to Washington's fabled foreign embassies in some of the finest old mansions in town. The Belgian Embassy, for instance, fills an entire block of fashionable Foxhall Road. Built by a former Nevada gold prospector and prison warden who became Woodrow Wilson's secretary of the U.S. Mint, the limestone château included a cold-storage room for rugs and furs, a refrigeration room for cut flowers, and a storage chamber specifically designed to hold bottled water. Villa Firenze, the Italian ambassador's residence on Albemarle Street, was once Robert and Polly Guggenheim's manor. Remarried to John Logan after Colonel Guggenheim's death, Polly sold the estate to the Italians. "We'll have to have a garage sale," she told the *Washington Star.* "A six-car garage sale."

Talk on the embassy circuit, and at power lunches elsewhere around town, is decidedly "Inside the Beltway." This refers not just to the sixty-six-mile expressway loop around the city, but also to insider political talk that consumes the local population and exasperates the rest of the nation. In power, out of power, plotting to regain power (Merriman Smith said it's a town where

Five National Theatres have occupied the same prominent site on Pennsylvania Avenue. In 1948, the National reopened as a movie house. It had closed as a legitimate theater to defray public pressure to integrate its audience. OPPOSITE: *General Haile Selassie bows to Jacqueline Kennedy as President John F. Kennedy waits to greet the Ethiopian emperor at Union Station. The private cars of many dignitaries have rolled into Washington's monolithic terminal.*

thousands of people never entirely unpack), local and national—all such lines are blurred when it comes to politics. Even suburbanites who shrug uninterestedly at the economic travails of their center city sit up and take notice when a delicious political fight is raging.

The liberal *Washington Post*, maybe most famous nationally for its journalists Bob Woodward and Carl Bernstein, who uncovered the Watergate scandal, covers it all. Its lone remaining daily competitor, the conservative *Washington Times*, hammers liberals and other Democrats and produces an estimable sports section. In Washington, national news is local news. In the 1990s, more than 80 percent of all District of Columbia workers brought home a federal or city government paycheck, delivered mail, lobbied Congress or other legislative agencies, or made a living in fields like environmental research whose financial pipeline led to Capitol Hill. Even local radio stations cover Capitol Hill, and area television stations send their own reporters to White House briefings and the news conferences of federal agencies and national organizations.

But the situation works in reverse as well: the television networks and other national media pounce on the story whenever Washington's financial and leadership kettle boils over. In 1995, for instance, President Clinton threw up his hands at the degree of the city's fiscal ineptitude and approved creation of a five-member control board. It was charged with balancing the city budget over four years, then seeing that it stayed balanced the next four—with or without the cooperation of the mayor and council. The president said he was looking for "a city that works" and called the measure Washington's "road back" from the brink of bankruptcy. Even the capital city's nonvoting delegate to the House of Representatives, Eleanor Holmes Norton, who had co-sponsored the bill, said it "quite literally saves the city." Chosen as chairman of the new oversight board was Andrew F. Brimmer, the son of a sharecropper who had been the first black governor of the Federal Reserve Board. The board was given authority to downsize city agencies, including the top-heavy school administration, and did so. Its enabling legislation directed the mayor to appoint a chief financial officer whom the control board must approve and only the control board could fire. Less than a year into the job, the CFO, Anthony A. Williams, told Congress that the city government was operating on such "lousy" day-to-day financial information that it would rate a "15 or 16" on a scale of 1 to 10, with 10 being the worst. Remarkably, all this dour activity seemed to energize D.C. business leaders and federal and city politicians alike. There was talk, if informal, about a new city charter, perhaps even a city manager form of government—anything to stop the hemorrhaging of dollars, middle-income taxpayers, and confidence in the capital city. Politicians of both national parties ruminated that Washington would be an ideal urban test tube, where chancy ideas like school vouchers, privatized city services, and enterprise zones might be explored. After all, what was there to lose?

As he signed the control-board legislation, President Clinton took pains to laud Washington as a city of magnificent neighborhoods worth saving. All cities have worthy neighborhoods, of course, but few with such diversity. A sampling: Georgetown, stately by day, "happening" at night. Foggy Bottom, an old German working-class neighborhood now subsumed by George Washington University halls, record stores, and restaurants. Southwest, whose neglected row houses and historic churches fell before bulldozers in a fit of urban renewal that turned much of the area into a wasteland of freeways and a "Federal Center" canyon of nondescript government buildings. Dupont Circle, Washington's fashionable in-town address to the northwest of the White House on the edge of "Embassy Row." Adams-Morgan, home to the heterogeneous and rapidly expanding Hispanic community. Shaw, once the heart of black enterprise and entertainment in segregated Washington and lively again with the reopening of the glamorous Lincoln Theater. And troubled Anacostia, isolated across the old Eastern Branch of the Potomac River, a dumping ground for many of the city's social problems and squalid public-housing projects. The Smithsonian Institution made a point of opening its Museum of African American History and Culture in Anacostia, and Marion Barry made a statement by moving into a house there.

Gone in Anacostia and swanky Chevy Chase alike as the twenty-first century neared were most old-line local banks and all the Washington savings and loans, merged into regional conglomerates. Woodward & Lothrup department store—"Woodies"—which had been a rock of local commerce for more than a century, became a memory. Utility firms went regional, and the business of Washington (other than politics) increasingly fell to real-estate developers, providers of professional services, and speculators in ventures like sushi bars and comedy clubs. With an eye toward the exploding research corridor out Interstate 270 in Montgomery County, Maryland, the Metropolitan Washington Council of Governments forecast steady growth to the year 2020 in engineering, computer and data processing, medical research, and other service fields. All in all as the millennium neared, optimism in beautiful Washington ran surprisingly high, even in the central city. "Race cards" were held closer to the vest, and sleeves were rolled up, on the theory that the only way for a city flat on its back to go was up.

OVERLEAF: Because Congress has held sway over the City of Washington, no high-rise buildings, save for the Washington Monument, were permitted to obscure the grandeur. So the city spread out rather than up. Where gargantuan government buildings now stretch toward the horizon, factories, churches, rooming houses, and even a rowdy neighborhood called "Murder Row" once stood. A fetid canal ran along what is now Constitution Avenue, railroad tracks and freight yards once cluttered the Mall, and squalid row houses reached almost to the Capitol.

ABOVE: Daniel Chester French designed the nineteen-foot-tall statue that is the centerpiece of the memorial to Abraham Lincoln.

Congress had incorporated a Lincoln Monument Association in 1867, but construction did not begin until 1914. President Lincoln's only surviving son,

Robert Todd Lincoln, was in attendance when the memorial, designed by architect Henry Bacon, was dedicated on May 30, 1922. OPPOSITE: Like a lighthouse, the

Washington Monument serves as a familiar beacon, visible from many corners of the city. It and other national landmarks, including the Lincoln

Memorial and U.S. Capitol, inspire poets, brighten the nighttime sky, and provide a memorable view for passengers descending into National Airport.

Architect Robert Mills's design for the Washington Monument called for a soaring obelisk and a circular, colonnaded "pantheon of heroes." General Washington was to be depicted riding a chariot. But when construction resumed in 1876 after a hiatus of many years, engineer Thomas Casey simplified the design and eliminated the pantheon. OPPOSITE: Because the Jefferson Memorial on the Potomac River Tidal Basin stands apart from other monuments, it draws fewer visitors than the Lincoln Memorial upriver.

When the cherry blossoms bloom in early spring, visitors and Washingtonians alike find an excuse to stroll the grounds along the Tidal Basin. The trees only sometimes oblige planners by timing their splendor to coincide with the city's famous Cherry Blossom Festival. ABOVE: Thomas Jefferson himself introduced the classical colonnade style into the new United States. So architect John Russell Pope borrowed the design for the memorial to Jefferson. Its walls are inscribed with some of Jefferson's writings. OVERLEAF: As seen from the tiny observation area of the Washington Monument, the Potomac River snakes past the Jefferson Memorial and National Airport on its way to the Chesapeake Bay. Not just autos but also Washington's sleek Metrorail transit cars whiz over the river to Alexandria and the airport.

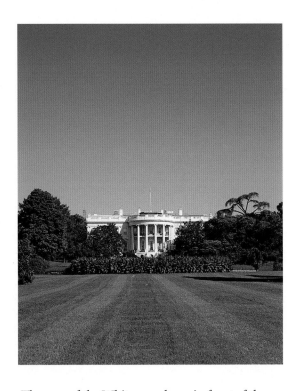

The rear of the White House, facing the Ellipse and less visible to the public than the 1600 Pennsylvania Avenue address around front, includes the Rose Garden, the windows of the elliptical Oval Office, and Harry Truman's second-story porch. Marine One, *the president's helicopter, lands on the South Lawn.* OPPOSITE: *A fresh snowfall coats the* lawn in front of the 132-room Executive Mansion. The president is rarely seen here, except to greet visiting dignitaries, though the family dining room—off limits to visitors— faces Pennsylvania Avenue. Concerns about the First Family's safety prompted the Secret Service to close this stretch of the avenue to vehicular traffic in 1995.

Alfred B. Mullett's Old Executive Office Building—the ornate, French Empire warren of offices for the president's staff—was detested when it was completed in 1888. When President William Howard Taft later named a Fine Arts Commission to plan new executive department buildings, Commissioner Cass Gilbert told a friend he hoped each chosen architect would be anything but "a cubist, a futurist, or a Mullett." Today, the chaotic building is much loved. ABOVE: Robert Mills, designer of the Washington Monument, also planned the enormous Treasury Building. Some say that President Jackson ordered it plunked where it is— blocking the vista to the Capitol—in a fit of pique against Congress. Truth was, Congress itself chose the site because it lay on cheap government land.

Guided tours of the Capitol usually begin beneath the dome, in the Rotunda. The dome's statue, Freedom, *is often mistaken for Pocahontas or another Native American figure. "Freedom" wears a helmet encrusted with stars, surmounted by an eagle's head and feathers. Inside the rotunda, Pocahontas is depicted in John G. Chapman's painting of her baptism.* Opposite: *The Capitol dome lights up the sky at dusk over busy Pennsylvania Avenue. The building's cast-iron dome is built in dual shells. It weighs nine million pounds and rises 285 feet above a hill that is already one of the highest spots in Washington. If a light is illuminated atop the dome, at least one body of Congress is in session. Clearing of the Mall ensured a relatively unobstructed view.*

The Capitol reflecting pool, added to the grounds in 1971, is presided over by a statue of Ulysses S. Grant. It offers a serene interlude between the frenzy inside the legislative chambers and the vigorous tenor of Independence, Constitution, and Pennsylvania avenues to the west. ABOVE: The Peace Monument, built in 1877, honors the U.S. Navy's Civil War dead. OVERLEAF: Constantino Brumidi's 1865 fresco, Apotheosis, is constructed in two rings—the inner representing the thirteen original states of the Union, and the outer depicting four hundred years of American history.

Carlo Franzoni's marble sculpture, Car of History, *stands at the north entrance of the Capitol's Statuary Hall, which served as the House chamber until 1857. Clio, the Muse of History,* stands in the car of Time, keeping track of events as they occur. Clockmaker Simon Willard designed the timepiece. It was once a congressional tradition to set this clock back as far as was deemed necessary to finish business before adjournment. OPPOSITE: As presiding officers of the Senate, vice-presidents of the United States are important ceremonial congressional figures. Although they are rarely in their seat in the Senate chamber, they have shown up to cast tie-breaking votes. Vice-presidents' busts line a hallway leading to the Senate chamber. Nearly every surface inside the public spaces of the Capitol—including each pedestrian corridor—is adorned with a magnificent painting, fresco, or bas-relief.

Alexander Hamilton's is one of the statues of great Americans in the Capitol Rotunda. Hamilton, the nation's first Treasury secretary, was a vocal supporter of a strong central government. He was shot by Thomas Jefferson's vice-president, Aaron Burr, in a duel in New Jersey on July 11, 1804, and died the next day. Underneath the Rotunda is an empty crypt that was set aside for the remains of George and Martha Washington, but never used. RIGHT: Portraits of the speakers of the House of Representatives line the wall of the Speaker's Lobby, just outside the House chamber.

Only the Library of Congress's most esteemed researchers have access to the Members' Room, whose ornamentation includes a marble fireplace topped by Frederick Dielman's mosaic depicting History with Mythology and Tradition.

America's oldest national cultural institution was opened in 1800 inside the U.S. Capitol. When most of its collection was destroyed by British torches in 1814, Thomas Jefferson sold to Congress (for $23,950) 6,487 of his personal works, in several languages. The collection has grown to well over one hundred million items, four-fifths in formats other than books.

OPPOSITE: The lavish Great Hall of the Jefferson Building was restored to mark the building's centennial in 1997. This sculpture by Philip Martiny stands at the foot of the Great Staircase. OVERLEAF: In the days when dozens of steam locomotives chugged past the Library's open windows on their way to Union Station, soot turned the Jefferson Building's magnificent artwork a dingy yellow, then almost black.

The aura of the United States Supreme Court Building is imposing, but it is among Washington's twenty top tourist sites. When the High Court convenes, visitors may hear a sample of lawyers' and justices' arguments in a brief walk-through. Or they may arrive early in hopes of securing one of the few seats available to the public for the entire day. Architect Cass Gilbert designed this legal temple after William Howard Taft, the only president to also serve as chief justice, pushed to get the justices a court-house of their own.

The Romanesque 1899 Old Post Office Building lasted as a post office only eighteen years. When postal workers moved to a site next to Union Station, the building became a storage facility, home to overflow federal offices. It was the city's most famous white elephant. Twice— when the massive Federal Triangle was built around it, and again in the 1970s— the "old tooth" was scheduled for demolition but survived.

ABOVE AND OPPOSITE: The Old Post Office is now a popular mall, filled with shops and restaurants. Inside and out, it is a place for fun.

A block of shops and small office buildings was razed to build the hulking $126-million FBI Building, which was immediately panned by architectural critics. One termed it "the Nightmare on Pennsylvania Avenue." The bureau's security-conscious director, J. Edgar Hoover—who himself called it ugly—permitted few entrances into his fortress, and street vendors were forbidden from setting up beneath it. LEFT: Michael Lantz's statue Man Controlling Trade sits outside the Federal Trade Commission Building at the apex of the Federal Triangle. Construction of the wall of the uniformly designed limestone buildings between the Mall and Pennsylvania Avenue was the largest public building project in American history.

ARCHIVES OF THE UNITED STATES OF AMERICA

When John F. Kennedy rode up Pennsylvania Avenue in his inaugural parade, he was aghast at its tackiness. "It's a disgrace," he is reported to have said. "Fix it." One of the results of a thirty-year makeover is tranquil Pershing Park (left), which is full of grasses, water lilies, and even lotuses in its pond. OPPOSITE: John Russell Pope designed the imposing National Archives Building more than a decade before he worked on the Jefferson Memorial. ABOVE: Robert Aitken's allegorical sculpture What Is Past Is Prologue greets Archives Building visitors.

Dry-goods dealers, tanners, several undertakers' offices, and two woolen mills once filled Market Square, across Pennsylvania Avenue from busy Center Market. As part of Pennsylvania Avenue's rebirth, Market Square came alive with twin neoclassical towers. Two separate projects included upscale housing units and restaurants that added energy and nightlife to the city's long-dormant main street.

ABOVE: The modest Navy Memorial fills Market Square's courtyard. A simple bronze Lone Sailor statue stands on a giant stone disk inscribed with a world map.

OVERLEAF: About 250,000 people, including veterans of all the nation's wars, are buried at Arlington National Cemetery, where an average of eighteen funerals are held each day.

The imposing statue of Union General John A. "Black Jack" Logan towers over the beautiful downtown circle that bears his name. ABOVE: The refurbished statue of Revolutionary War hero Casimir Pulaski, in his Polish marshal's uniform, stands before the Old Post Office Building. OVERLEAF: The inspirational U.S. Marine Corps Memorial is found in Northern Virginia, just north of Arlington Cemetery. Felix de Weldon executed the bronze statue from Joe Rosenthal's famous photograph of the triumphant raising of the flag on Mount Suribachi on Iwo Jima during World War II.

Maya Ying Lin,
a Yale University
architecture student,
designed "The Wall"
at the Vietnam
Veterans Memorial
(above). Friends and
loved ones often make
tracings from the
more than 58,000
names etched into the
wall. Or they leave
poignant souvenirs,
some of which are
displayed at the
Smithsonian Institu-
tion's National
Museum of American
History. LEFT:
Eleven years after
the completion of the
Vietnam Veterans
Memorial, a Vietnam
Women's Memorial
(© 1993, V.W.M.P.,
Inc.; Glenna Good-
acre, sculptor)
was added nearby.
It depicts two uni-
formed women
caring for a wounded
male soldier.

67

In 1995, the Korean War Veterans Memorial (© KWVM Productions, Inc.) was unveiled across the Mall reflecting pool from the Vietnam Veterans Memorial. Highlighting the timeless theme "Freedom Is Not Free," the memorial was designed by Washington's Cooper•Lecky Architects. It depicts nineteen battle-clad, stainless-steel troopers, created by Frank Gaylord, warily venturing into the open and heading for a giant American flag. To their side is a black granite wall, designed by Louis Nelson Associates, into which are etched the faces of more than twenty-five hundred support troops, taken from photographs. ABOVE: Each trooper wears a heavy poncho—standard issue for Korea's heavy rains and bitter cold.

Robert Berks's memorial to Albert Einstein stands outside the National Research Council building. The granite figure holds a tablet showing three of his important equations, including one that summarizes the theory of general relativity. BOTTOM: The statue of Mary McLeod Bethune rests opposite an emancipation monument in Lincoln Park off East Capitol Street. Also executed by Robert Berks, it was commissioned by the National Council of Negro Women, which Bethune founded. OPPOSITE: A third Berks work, the bust of President John F. Kennedy, dominates the lobby of the Kennedy Center for the Performing Arts. Its six theaters present more musical and artistic performances than any other single institution in the nation. OVERLEAF: The Smithsonian's sandstone "Castle" building on the Washington Mall houses the visitor center for the vast scientific institution.

MARY McLEOD BETHUNE
1875 1955
Let her works praise her

"Meet me at the elephant" is a familiar refrain among families who visit the museums on the Washington Mall. This beast is the centerpiece of the Smithsonian Institution's National Museum of Natural History. The remains of thousands more creatures help depict the history of the natural world and human cultures. ABOVE: One of the most enduringly popular Smithsonian exhibits is the array of First Ladies' formal gowns, displayed at the National Museum of American History, which also examines American artifacts as mundane as the bicycle and washing machine. OVERLEAF: Known for its rockets, space capsules, and thrilling IMAX movies, the Air and Space Museum also displays the most vintage of all aircraft, the Wright Brothers' Flyer.

Futuristic architect I. M. Pei designed the East Building of the National Gallery of Art, where the gallery's modernist holdings are most often exhibited. The building, whose layout looks like a piece of a cubist jigsaw puzzle, stands in stark contrast to John Russell Pope's classical, domed West Building, which was a gift to the nation from financier Andrew Mellon. ABOVE: The art is almost indefinable at the Smithsonian Institution's Hirshhorn Museum of Contemporary Art, which wags have called "the Doughnut on the Mall." It includes a sunken sculpture garden. The museum is named for Joseph Hirshhorn, a Latvian immigrant who made a fortune mining uranium and donated thousands of paintings, drawings, and sculptures to the Smithsonian.

One of the lesser-known Smithsonian galleries is the National Museum of American Art, removed from the Mall in the Gallery Place–Chinatown neighborhood across Pennsylvania Avenue. It features American paintings, sculpture, graphics, folk art, and photography of the eighteenth century to the present. BOTTOM: The Renwick Gallery is an offshoot of the National Museum of American Art. Also located some distance from the Mall, across the street from the White House, it displays American crafts. OPPOSITE: The Smithsonian's National Portrait Gallery shares the old Patent Office Building with the National Museum of American Art. When Robert Mills finished the huge quadrangular structure in 1867, it was the largest building in the country. The gallery displays the portraits of distinguished Americans like George Washington and features a Civil War exhibition.

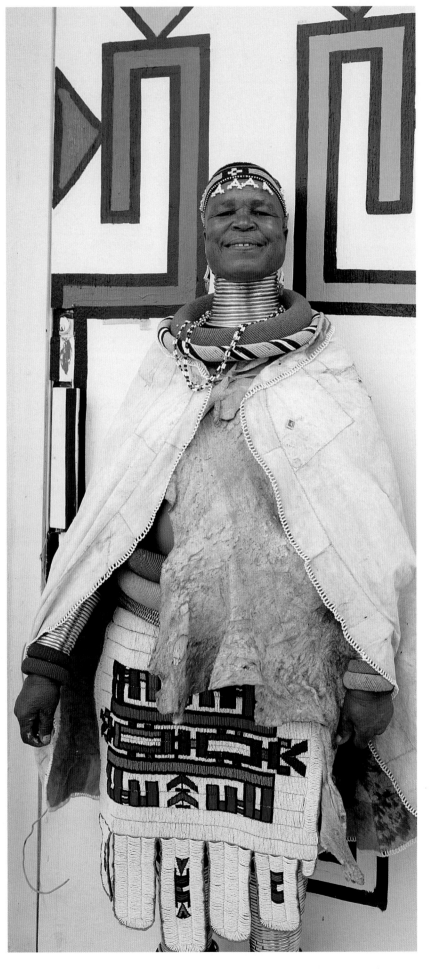

The National Museum of African Art (above), behind the "Castle," is another Smithsonian gallery. It holds more than six thousand works of traditional art from sub-Saharan Africa. RIGHT: South African muralist Esther Mahlangu created a Ndebele wall painting on a façade of the annex of the National Museum of Women in the Arts, on New York Avenue. OPPOSITE: The United States Holocaust Memorial Museum displays disturbing reminders of a barbaric chapter in world history. But it also recalls more sanguine times in the lives of Holocaust victims. OVERLEAF: Columns removed from the U.S. Capitol form an imposing peristyle at the 444-acre United States National Arboretum, which includes the National Bonsai Collection and the National Herb Garden.

The United States
Botanic Gardens
(above) are a tropical
paradise of orchids,
cacti, ferns, and other
exotic plants in the
shadow of the Capitol.
Seasonal displays are
featured in the conser-
vatory and across
Independence Avenue
in a beautiful formal
outdoor garden.
RIGHT: Rock Creek
Park's 1,800 acres
extend from George-
town in the heart of
the city far out into
Montgomery County,
Maryland. They
encompass fifteen
miles of hiking trails
(with exercise
stations), a golf course
and horse center, bike
paths, picnic areas,
and the Smithsonian's
National Zoo.
The National Park
Service rangers also
frequently present
special children's
activities, music,
arts, and crafts.
Each spring, the hill-
sides erupt into a
stunning panorama
of daffodils.

Franklin Square provides an oasis in the K Street business corridor. High-powered lawyers, lobbyists, and stock-brokers break for lunch in the park over which Prentiss Properties' classic 1301 K Street Towers looms. ABOVE: The smaller McPherson Square is two blocks west. Union General James B. McPherson died in the capture of Atlanta. OVERLEAF: Pershing Park offers a serene view of the Willard Hotel, which has stood at this location since 1816. Derelict and aban-doned, its furnish-ings sold at auction in 1969, the Willard was eventually saved by stubborn citizens and the Pennsylva-nia Avenue Develop-ment Corporation.

Interior designer
Sarah Tomerlin Lee
of New York toured
the vacant Willard
Hotel in 1983 and
likened it to "the ruins
of the Baths of Cara-
calla." Columns and
mosaic floors had been
destroyed, rats the size
of cats frolicked in
Peacock Alley, and
holes in the walls were
so enormous, you
could watch cars go
past. RIGHT: The
Willard was restored
by the Oliver T. Carr
Company. Its ornate
lobby features
columns revived with
an imitation marble
called scagliola.
OVERLEAF: The fash-
ionable Watergate
Hotel, on the Potomac
River, was the site of
the infamous break-in
of the Democratic
National Committee
by White House
"plumbers" in 1972.
Some of Washington's
wealthiest and most
powerful citizens
keep apartments at
the Watergate,
and several nations
use it as their
embassy address.

Not just monumental Washington is stunningly beautiful. So are many revitalized office buildings. The John Akridge Company's Homer Building (right) reshaped a declining neighborhood around Metro Center, at the juncture of three Metro subway lines. The restored original lobby leads into a striking atrium that features Donald Harcourt DeLue's sculpture Spirit of American Youth. The building once housed the S. Kann department store. ABOVE: The grand cruciform at 1001 Pennsylvania Avenue caught the eye of the producers of the 1987 Hollywood film Broadcast News. Tenants were the extras as William Hurt and Jack Nicholson scurried in and out. The precast aluminum clock was made in Salt Lake City.

Georgetown Park (left), at Wisconsin Avenue and M Street in the heart of one of the city's most popular shopping neighborhoods, is one of Washington's most stylish arcades. International tourists, in particular, seem to gravitate to Georgetown Park, which Fodor's travel guide described as looking like "a Victorian ice-cream parlor." Come December, a stroll through the mall is like a walk through a Dickens Christmas past. ABOVE: Georgetown opted against a Metro subway stop, so the trains rumble past into Virginia, where the Fashion Centre mall thrives at Pentagon City. Just south of the Pentagon itself, the indoor mall serves a 116-acre "mixed-use" Arlington County neighborhood that includes high-rise office and apartment buildings, a large hotel, a nursing home, and parks. Its success was assured when it got its own Metro subway stop on lines to Alexandria and National Airport.

Architect Daniel Burnham's passion for natural light is evident in the remodeled West Hall of Union Station. Where passengers once checked bags in the old terminal— and grime obscured the skylight as the station fell to ruin— there's now an upscale shopping arcade. Here, each Christmas, is a fabulous miniature-train display. And real long-distance, commuter, and local trains still roll into the dazzlingly refurbished landmark. RIGHT: Metro, which reaches into the suburbs like an octopus from the city's central core, has been a stunning success—a tourist attraction unto itself. Police patrols and vigilance by passengers have kept the trains clean and remarkably crime- and graffiti-free.

Work began on the Washington National Cathedral (left), the world's sixth-largest cathedral, in 1907 and took eighty-three years to complete. The Episcopal Church oversees the Gothic cathedral, but several denominations hold services there. OPPOSITE: The peal of bells from the National Shrine of the Immaculate Conception can be heard across the campus of the Catholic University of America and beyond. Every parish in the nation contributed to the construction of America's largest Catholic church. OVERLEAF: The illuminated tower of the Temple of the Church of Jesus Christ of Latter-Day Saints, topped by the statue of the Mormon angel Moroni, is a landmark along the Capital Beltway in suburban Maryland. Once, a brazen thief in a helicopter tried unsuccessfully to wrench the golden statue from its moorings.

OPPOSITE: *The nondenominational Howard University Divinity School, which dates to 1870, is now housed in a former Franciscan seminary building designed by architect Chester Oakley. The figure at the left is Saint Bonaventure, a thirteenth-century Italian priest who became minister general of the Franciscan order. To his right is a rendering of John Duns Scotus, a Scottish-born medieval theologian and philosopher.*

LEFT: *Once a combination classroom-dormitory at the National Deaf-Mute College, architect J. D. Meyers's 1877 College Hall at Gallaudet University now houses the president's and other administrative offices. President Lincoln signed the bill establishing a college for hard-of-hearing students in 1864. Named for its first president, Edward Miner Gallaudet, and originally all-male, it first admitted women in 1887.*

The Gothic spires of Georgetown University (left), the nation's oldest Jesuit school, tower above the Georgetown neighborhood. The outstanding reputation of the university's medical, international relations, and law schools reaches worldwide. ABOVE: *The intersection of Wisconsin Avenue and M Street is the city's oldest, dating to the period when Georgetown was a thriving port, before the capital was moved to the new city of Washington. The gold dome of the Riggs National Bank Building has long been a landmark on the northeast corner.* OVERLEAF: *The Chesapeake and Ohio Canal was once navigable all the way to Cumberland, Maryland. Its towpath remains a popular hiking and biking trail.*

The gardens of Mount Vernon, President Washington's Potomac River estate, are legendary. Washington was his own landscape architect. He often wrote home to instruct groundskeepers in the gardens' care. In his diary, he once noted, "Road to my Mill Swamp . . . in search of the sort of Trees I shall want for my Walks, groves and Wildernesses." ABOVE: The nucleus of the Mount Vernon mansion was constructed about 1735 by Washington's father, Augustine. Fourteen rooms, containing numerous original furnishings, are open for viewing. When the Mount Vernon Ladies' Association bought and saved the estate in 1858, it inspired the American preservation movement. The estate, south of Alexandria, Virginia, along a scenic parkway, is reachable by automobile, bus connection to the Metro subway, the Washington Tourmobile, and even by boat.

Quaint Alexandria, Virginia (above), was a thriving port when the capital was moved to Washington. It was incorporated inside the new District of Columbia, but later ceded back to Virginia. RIGHT: Capitol Hill is a neighborhood of brownstones and other pricey row houses, many of which have been divided into apartments to house the never-ending stream of eager new congressional aides. OPPOSITE: Colorful Adams-Morgan is a multicultural neighborhood that is home to some of the city's hottest restaurants and festivals. Hispanics, in particular, from dozens of countries, gravitate to this lively neighborhood.

There is a National Historic Site in Washington's Anacostia neighborhood, marking the home of abolitionist Frederick Douglass. But he is remembered elsewhere as well, as in this Massachusetts Avenue mural. Douglass created the Freedman's Savings Bank during the Civil War for the use of black Union troops and former slaves. RIGHT: Sixteenth Street, leading uptown directly from the White House, was once the city's most fashionable address. It was the first Embassy Row before many nations built even more impressive mansions along Massachusetts Avenue. Even tattered by age and mistreatment, the magnificent brownstones farther up Sixteenth, Fourteenth, and Thirteenth streets recall a gentler age of gaslights and surreys.

Ben's Chili Bowl is an institution in the old Shaw neighborhood, once the heart of black enterprise in segregated Washington. Several building associations promoted home ownership, and thus stability, there. Sensational musical clubs and dance halls, including the Lincoln Colonnade, were clustered along U Street.
Bottom: *Even in the blight of Washington's Far Southeast neighborhood, great Depression-era artwork survives.*
Opposite: *Thirteenth Street is another radial where gracious old homes have survived. The street, which changes names as it winds into suburban Maryland, has become a commuter corridor.*
Overleaf: *Washington's Chinatown is small but vigorous. Its colorful, seventy-five-foot-wide Friendship Arch spans H Street at Seventh Street, not far from the site of the MCI Center sports arena.*

The patio of the Spanish ambassador's residence on Sixteenth Street is an imitation of an Andalusian courtyard, with its window ironwork, tiled floor, fountain, and portrait of the Blessed Virgin. The embassy is housed in Boundary Castle, a turreted brownstone once owned by Mary Foote Henderson, whom the Washington Star *called "Washington's social arbiter."* Above: *The music* room of the Mexican Cultural Institute features an organ and Louis XIII-style chair. The home on Sixteenth Street was built by a "mystery owner," who turned out to be William Howard Taft's secretary of the Treasury, Franklin MacVeagh. MacVeagh presented it to his wife, Emily, as a Christmas gift. Today the institute offers cultural programs and art exhibitions.

It was one of a dozen separate buildings that Henderson commissioned architect George Oakley Totten Jr. to build as potential embassy sites in "Washington Heights." Above: *The music*

Marble dancers on the Y-shaped grand staircase of the Indonesian Embassy beckon to a promenade gallery leading to second-floor suites. The building, on Massachusetts Avenue, was constructed by Tom Walsh, a Colorado gold prospector who struck it rich. His drawing room now holds the instruments of a traditional Indonesian gamelin orchestra. OPPOSITE: The Japanese ambassador's residence on Nebraska Avenue contains both contemplative and functional spaces. Eight landscape architects constructed the gardens and pond. OVERLEAF: No embassy is better known for its gardens than the "Chancery and Residence of the Ambassador of the United Kingdom of Great Britain and Northern Ireland," on Massachusetts Avenue. One of the city's hottest diplomatic invitations is a summons to the British Embassy for strawberries, cream, and champagne to toast the monarch's birthday.

Index

"George Washington," one of the Time Travelers troupe of historical interpreters, greets a girl on Pennsylvania Avenue's Western Plaza. The name was later changed to "Freedom Plaza" to honor Dr. Martin Luther King Jr. A time capsule containing items of Dr. King's is buried in the plaza on Pennsylvania Avenue.

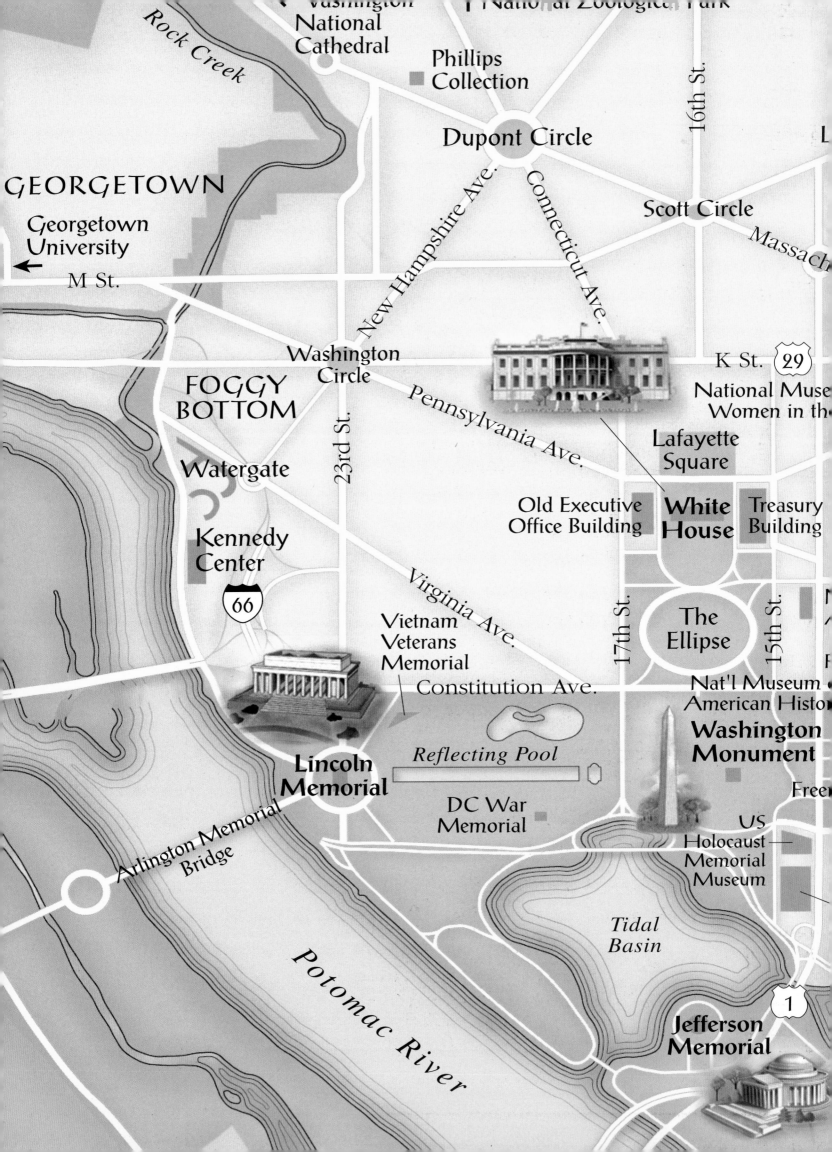

Rock Creek

Washington
National
Cathedral

National Zoological Park

Phillips
Collection

16th St.

Dupont Circle

GEORGETOWN

Scott Circle

Georgetown
University

Massach

M St.

New Hampshire Ave.

Connecticut Ave.

K St. 29

Washington
Circle

National Muse
Women in the

FOGGY
BOTTOM

Pennsylvania Ave.

Lafayette
Square

Watergate

23rd St.

Old Executive
Office Building

**White
House**

Treasury
Building

Kennedy
Center

66

Virginia Ave.

17th St.

The
Ellipse

15th St.

Vietnam
Veterans
Memorial

Constitution Ave.

Nat'l Museum
American Histor

**Washington
Monument**

**Lincoln
Memorial**

Reflecting Pool

DC War
Memorial

Free

US

Arlington Memorial
Bridge

Holocaust
Memorial
Museum

*Tidal
Basin*

Potomac River

1

**Jefferson
Memorial**